there are boxes and there is wanting

Dawn —
thank you for being
the kind of poet who
made me want to write
+ put that writing
into the world.

⌐

there are boxes and there is wanting by Tessa Micaela Landreau-Grasmuck
Published by Trembling Pillow Press
New Orleans, LA
ISBN-13: 978-0996475709
Copyright © 2016 by Tessa Micaela Landreau-Grasmuck

Typesetting and Design: Megan Burns
Author Photo: Brittany Billmeyer-Finn
Cover Design: JS Makkos
Photograph: Nihil Minus

Trembling
Pillow
PRESS

there are boxes and there is wanting

by Tessa Micaela Landreau-Grasmuck

Bob Kaufman (1925-1986)
detail of woodcut by Kristin Wetterhahn

WINNER OF THE 2015 BOB KAUFMAN BOOK PRIZE
SELECTED BY LAURA MULLEN

there are boxes and there is wanting

preface:
on refusing to say what it is

we are precarious bodies. we are precarious bodies beneath reinforced structures. and so we are precarious amongst families and fictions and economies and illnesses.

our bodies are ticking and we are trying to breathe. we are living between days and nights and they are precarious. and so our bodies are flooded and drowning beside the waterways.

we wake up thirsty and go for days without looking at the sky or noticing the clusters of trees. when we didn't look there was a ring that formed around the fallen trunks that have burst into flame and covered our lungs in ash. all around our bodies and inside of our bodies are agencies and coastlines, and trees and breathing. the trees and the breathing are a set of intermingling stories. the agencies and the coasts are a set of disrupting stories. they each represent themselves, and they each represent other things.

toward the beginnings or the ends, when we might become aware of the light or the dark depending on the time of night, and depending on the sounds that may or may not always be around us, like bottles breaking or highways, we begin to tell a story. i begin to tell a story, because it is mine. i begin to tell a story and stop, because it is not only mine.

we want to know what happened. we want to know when and where, what it looked like and who did what. we want to know simply and without excuse. except, sometimes the best way to tell what happened is not always to tell it. there are always things left out. like, our bodies are individual and there is plenty of water. like, this is a story about the world we live in or this is a story about what happened inside a house. like, the world and the house are separate from one another. like, our bodies are snarling and the differences between us are sets of stories.

and so we begin again and begin again, despite the storms. it has taken all we had to keep going, and we do, even if we are swirling downward. at least we are dancing. at least we are not separate from one another.

crossings are never undertaken all at once and never once and for all.

[m. jacqui alexander]

beginning on a stage

there are these things:

there is red and there is red and there is red that faces into the edge of the landmass and then there is blue and there is blue and there is waiting.

beneath the sifted and packed rock is a sky and a series of thorns. and if there is listening to what is beneath even this, there is fire and there is fire and then the seeds open and gather marrow.

all the characters who arrive have something to do with this fire and these groves, even if they've never been to this place or have no memory of having arrived.

there are these things: there is blue and there is blue and there is blue at the edge of the coastline and then there is green and there is green and there is wanting.

none of this is outside the body   if the body doesn't end at the skin.

enter character carrying a book

the body is made up of millions of smaller structures that carry on a host of different activities. but, and this being an important point, together all of these diverse activities accomplish the one big, all-encompassing function of the body - survival.

we are swimming. we try to swim the 60 miles to the coast. we've tried twice before and we try it again. during the day we swim and at night we sleep in the boat that floats beside the water. this year we can't reach the coast because of a new breed of jellyfish in the warming waters. because the warming waters are awash in jellyfish which sting us all over our bodies for endless days. they sting us and our heart leaps. they sting us and the others pull us out of the water in respiratory shock. at night, when we sleep in the boat, others photograph the bodies swollen and covered in welts. to document the warming waters. to document the bodies.

we are swimming.

our fears are about exiting.

enter character dressed in green

the force-field of the body extends four feet in all directions.

a good medicine also includes a delivery system, something that gets it to the parts of the body that need it.

i want to show them how i can always get up and walk away.

i want to show them that it isn't my ailing body that i am thinking about.

it isn't that these separate stories are one and the same. it is that they cannot be pulled apart from one another. it is that there are agencies all across and underneath and inside the bodies that exist inside the agencies. it is that there are agencies and that they are not separate from these stories. or these families.

we are surrounded by water and in being so we are unreasonably affected by the tides and all the drowning.

it looks different depending on the view. depending on the view there is devastation. there are bodies piecing each other back together. say the bodies were dismembered by other bodies. say remember, or say memory is marked in marrow. say crossing over. say nightingale.

there is a patient.

there is a patient
inside of a room.

there is a patient
inside of a white room
with an expressionless face.

the patient writes lists
on the walls of the white room.

the patient reads lists
from the walls of the white room.
the patient reads from the walls
in a voice that does not break.

since being inside the room,
the patient has developed
an increasing tendency
to curl inward.

outside the room
the patient leans against
large boulders.
the patient leans
against chain-link fences.

since being let out
of the white room,
the patient has developed
a shuffling walk.

the patient is told
they are alone inside the room,
and even more alone
outside the room,
but the patient
does not always believe
what they are told.

the patient sees many others
with a shuffling walk
and many others
who curl inward.

there is a patient.

there is how they see themselves
and how they are seen.

the patient walks in a forest
close to a shoreline.

around them are beginnings and endings.
some are visible, while some are not.
around them is fire and water.

the patient has a family.

each member of the family
has seven generations of children
marked along the marrow.

there are stories
each generation
tells the next.
they include how to walk
along crowded streets,
and who not to become.

in each generation,
certain ones have benefited
from these stories
while certain others
have fallen beneath.

it is usually the same kinds of falling
in proportion to the benefits.

when the patient arrives home
they are the most able of the bunch.

and everyone plays along
pretending they are not a patient
because that way
all the arrangements
stay in order.

i am here, they say,
ill-fitted inside their trachea,

their wings caught and clipped.

there is a patient.

there is a patient
inside of a white room.

between the white walls of the room,
the patient shreds faded pages.
the patient carves tiny tunnels
through the stacks of paper.
paper which tells something about results
and something about predispositions,
paper marked with ink
that takes the patient away
without saying their name.

between the white walls of the room,
the patient begins to sew
and blue silk thread folds
and reaches the length of the arm,
the arm raised in tiny punctuations of the room,
the room becoming blue and silken,
and splintering along the edges,
the edges touched by arms
reaching and folding blue.

inside the white room
silken letters reach sideways
and wind around the ill-fitted patient,
ill-fitted sewing and tearing
with organs and tentacles and wings
beneath the soft white bones,
bones stained grey
from the first dose of relief,
relief from what already was,
or what was made, ill-fitted.

there is a patient
in a now empty room
filled with shredded pages
and ill-fitted names.

there is a patient.

the patient is told
that they have a body
all to themselves.
they are told to let other people
touch that body.
they are told their body
is not a part of
other people's bodies.
they are told
that their body is different
from the bodies that have fallen beneath.
they are told that their body
is the same as all the other bodies.

it is then they begin to become invisible.

this is a story: down the hall the nurse hears someone calling out help me, help me, but can't go help because there aren't enough nurses. no one goes to help and the calling goes on for over an hour. there aren't enough nurses, and the ones that are there work themselves to the bone and still down the hall someone calls out for help.

this is another story: a man who works from six am to two pm, takes a nap, and wakes up again to work from ten pm to four am. he naps again and repeats. we predict that he won't be a very old man. he doesn't have a doctor and if he did the doctor would tell him that he had a weak heart. we think that if he let himself admit his sadness something might run down his left arm and leave him. or enter him.

the most apparent symptom of trauma transference is hyper-vigilance. it's why so many of us have a hard time keeping our footing.

this is a story: don't come up behind me.

enter character in search of a past

driving along the coast the coast
turning a bend a sharp bend the
coast turning around a sharp
bend a figure pulling a shopping
cart a figure cloaked in white a
figure in the middle of the road
in the middle of the bend in the
road ocean against the cliff the
cliff here beside the road the cliff
which drops off into the ocean
the face covered the face wrapped
in white it is evening and growing
into night slowing down suddenly
at least ten miles until a pull off
until a place to lay and sleep it is
growing into night will the figure
around the bend the figure in
white will she sleep in the middle
of the road in the middle of the
road face covered in white all
covered in white slowing to pass
eyes catch do not stop eyes catch
the eyes on the face covered in
white and no one says it may not
be all human the cliff falling off
beside the road and no place to
stop pulling a cart in the middle
of the road around a bend face
covered bandaged eyes catch do
not stop the middle of the curving
road cliffs above the water pulling
a cart and shoeless all around her
was the color of do not stop we
are not wanted there is something
other worldly do not stop it is not
safe gained speed and others saw
her and yes could not stop did not
stop and will not someone says
wanders the coast the face covered
masked in white two holes for eyes
holes for eyes for eyes unwhole.

enter character whispering

the sky is wild and i watch it.

enter character dressed in green

one of the first things is to attack the sense of history of those they wish to dominate by attempting to take over and control their relationships to their own past. it always requires some kind of replacement origin myth: a story that explains the new imbalances as natural, inevitable and permanent, as somehow inherent to the natures of invader and invaded and therefore unchangeable.

those crossing the coast at night drown in the waters, and drown having no water. we are listening for the trucks driving by and thinking about who is watching.

among the things we find riding through the dry shrubs and channels on the shoreline is a plastic bag of children's shoes and a ladder. we are always wishing, especially when we aren't the ones who climb or are drowned.

enter character in search of a past

i've been dreaming:

i install a filtration system in a deep
pool. the pool is in a large room. the
room has a familiar smell. all the
people who have come here, have come
because it is night and because we are
not supposed to be here and everyone
is laughing. all the people who have
come jump into the deep pool. i pause
for a moment. i pause long enough to
suddenly wonder why all the ones who
jumped in aren't coming back up, but i
don't pause long enough to stop myself
from jumping in after. underwater
there is this pulling and this dragging
and we are hauled toward the cluster
of other bodies. the crowd of people
is pushing back against the suction
that is pulling us into its bowels. all
of our feet are against the grate or
against each other's backs, and it is
the filtration system holding us pinned
as we are also weightless. all of us
pushing back against each other but
we are stuck against and underwater
and cannot breath and overpowered
and we are ended.

then there is an explosion and we are forced away, circling and wildly toward the top. and then the water clears and only some of us are on the surface and bodies standing on the bottom of the pool wearing red shirts and breathless. we already see from far above, that some of us are laid down, and there are not enough of us on the surface, and breathless, we reenter to pull them out. not enough breathing, and as we reach the bottom to pull the rest of us to the top it is suddenly night all around me and there is an unfamiliar smell, and i feel, still, along an edge and not breathing, and again there is no recovery from such consequences of waiting, having paused but not having paused long enough.

enter character carrying a book

every disease has different signs and symptoms. some include: persistent headache, loss of feeling, memory loss, loss of muscle strength, tremors, seizures, and slurred speech. one should seek medical attention if affected by these. causes include trauma, infections, degeneration, structural defects, tumors, autoimmune disorders. there is a wide variety of treatments. these can range from surgery to rehabilitation or prescribed medications.

enter character whispering

i had my hands grabbed.

i had the instinct to collapse.

enter character in search of a past

my whole face was crying but i wasn't feeling any emotions they say shame isn't an emotion it's a distortion it was as if i had a heater on inside a doctor touched my palm it's hot and wet she said your nervous system is overloaded and compensating no shit i didn't say and let her touch me my hands weeping as her fingers touched my throat which bothered me not because i've ever been strangled well not in this body in other bodies i've been killed by asphyxiation and self-imposed suffocation of the airway and i can remember somehow without having any way to picture my remembering like how i remember being a mother but how i haven't been and in dreams a sound whacks against the inside of a ceramic bowl and everybody pretends to believe it isn't this way but it is and outside two men are arguing until their throats are scraping the glass but my turn to speak forgoes a doorway.

enter character dressed in green

there again is this question of evidence, biology, energetic fields. we got some place to sleep passing through a small town. after the bars closed the doors opened in the room where we were curled in the corner and everybody was too drunk to realize the same song was playing for the fifth time. when everybody went outside to smoke a cigarette the old man who owned the bar held down the head of the drunk woman and it was clear she didn't like it and in the corner summoning the courage to get up and say something and then everybody came back in and she says i can't believe he made me suck his and we are still in the corner pretending to be asleep.

enter character dressed in green

in a rusted iron field a storm started. we are not trying to wait all night in the roadside bathroom and anyway this highway is cowardly. macerated and unrecognizable.

official policies do not explain stripping them down to their underwear in the cold while waiting for a train or a bus to arrive and the last thing to be refused is a meal or a glass of water. often it feels like someone caught hold and won't let go. like the shape of a body with its arms stretched out. made masked. made unrecognizable.

enter character whispering

there is a house on the horizon.

it has roots.

there are boxes

enter character in search of a past

someone is killing my mother. she doesn't know it and i don't know it for sure and my brother doesn't know it at all. but someone is killing my mother. take a look at her internal organs.

say the view was undisturbed.

say malnutrition.

say age. say war.

say what wars are unseen.

mourn them.

mourn face, its disappearance.

say disappearance.

repeat.

any investigation of skin must start here. it must start in the present in order to seek ways of connecting to the past. it must start in the acknowledgment of the fact that skin matters, matters viscerally, and in different ways. it must begin in an acknowledgment of the different shades, textures, and feel of skin, of skin as testimony both to the subjective state of individuals and to the histories that have molded them.

my brother's heart was exfoliated back to the blue.

it isn't mine to tell. and what is mine to tell includes the parts i don't want to expose. because i can't calculate the cost of telling it like it is. and to whom. because chemical dispositions and misdiagnoses in adolescence do not make a story. a brother who became a stranger and this not being the first time this has happened in a family is not a story. that there was hardly a beginning and too many centers and having an end in sight not being a luxury we've ever afforded does not make a story. which leads to my sense of not being able to tell what is and is not mine. as the events were cumulative and disassociated, and i can't remember most of them without a flood of all the other events that may or may not mean anything if you don't know the other sets of events. like seeing him walking down 23rd street alone, almost running, with a half-smile, half-panicked look on his face after having said he was going out to the north and was walking south. like how i was driving by looking at him in the mirror and did not stop, feeling worried and afraid and implicated and never telling anyone that i didn't want to have the feeling of knowing so much and never telling anyone that i was planning on disappearing so as to not have to pick up any more metaphorical pieces. it isn't a story to see my brother walking down the street alone and it isn't a story to have feelings about it. the look on his face and me not stopping is not a story. our lives after he was no longer the child-brother and how i try and trace back to remember a set of moments that might have been the causes or the cracks but despite all the blaming there aren't any beginnings just a whole lot of endings.

i'm not going to tell the story of being in and beside and surrounded and choked by illnesses that have no symptoms but are nonetheless of the body, his body as much as my body as much as all the bodies that led down or across or up to us. i am not going to tell about siblings that carry within them the cellular markings of the others. amidst all the not knowing what was next and choking and looking, there was always a long list of reasons and there were never any conclusions, just exacerbations. my brother left while everyone was out on a walk. he left a note that said, don't worry it's just that you can't understand my silence, but before he left the little girls had become scared. later, he yelled into my ear receiver, if you weren't so fucking sensitive i wouldn't have to yell like this, i wouldn't have to leave like this if everyone wasn't so fucking scared. when it is at its most quiet i worry about what happens as things are left alone to spin and i don't tell anyone because there is no story to tell. the little girls were frightened. a tree climbs through the walls of the house and blooms through the ceiling. my brother leans against my arm and is a glass bottle. by this i mean: it is always more than what it looks like.

often the marks that are overlooked are the ones without events.

the ones inside of a house.

or, the house is open to visitors who won't look too closely.

or, for years the house wondered what might happen next,

and if all the occupants would be alive the next day.

this is not an exaggeration.

this is a story:

i run room to room wondering when the stairs will appear.

the drawers i have looked to open were locked,

while others were spilled all across the floor.

toward the water we arrive halfway but don't go.

this is another story:

my brother is ill. what he has, by definition,

is resistant to being defined. there is what can be known

and what cannot be known

and when it was really ugly we shut the front door.

it's colder now, so we stay still.

i was eavesdropping and agreed when the one speaking said, i want to be a parent but i don't want to be a mother. my brother uses ours as a mirror. that's what she says anyway, and then fights not to bite his hooks, knowing what can't be known and not knowing how to let go. and with all the falling how can she, but how can she keep holding on, so tired and getting weak. sometimes i catch her sitting in the dark in front of the mirror saying, find someone who doesn't have these genes so it won't all happen again. she doesn't really say that, she says, your brother isn't the same as my sister, but i still answer the phone on instinct.

it's my father who says the things that aren't to be repeated. when he does i want to slam my hands over his mouth but i look down at the grass and choke. then the dog brings back the tennis ball that we'd tossed across the night.

when i say choke i mean the knots in the family begin wrapping around the neck. this before everyone went in opposite directions and if we'd kept going, we would have met on the other side. it's easier to think of things that way, meeting on the other side. where there might be less space to say but more ways of saying and the story could go on being told. we've left my father alone for a while, so he takes his shoes off at the door and doesn't turn on the lights. when he's angry he waves his arms and he waves his voice. with no one home he doesn't realize he is angry. even if he did, there is nothing to be done. i wave my arms when i am sleeping and see faces there and then i realize my hands are wet; they are weeping. i find myself asking the dark to stay where it is, where it is warm and the walls shake only a few times a night and this bleeding means that, for now, there are no visible wounds.

then it was dark and the animals were running

in the grass and we looked

toward the streetlights lining the highway and said help

as we did not say it.

something was there,

something like being afraid of the night staying

or the quick shadows in the field.

enter character carrying a book

this test is designed to help you understand:

i nearly always feel "empty." i find that i often do one or more of the following: drive recklessly, engage in unsafe sex, abuse alcohol or drugs, binge eat, gamble, or spend money recklessly. i often idealize others, especially when i first meet them. i often experience a sudden shift in the way i look at myself and my life, and completely change my goals, values, and career focus. sometimes when i'm stressed out, especially if someone has abandoned me, i can get very paranoid, feel myself "spacing out." i'm often afraid that others will abandon or leave me, so i'll make frantic efforts to avoid this abandonment. i have a hard time controlling my anger. my views of others - especially those i care about - can shift dramatically and without any warning. my mood can shift between extreme periods of anxiety, depression, or irritability in just a few hours or days. i've engaged in self-mutilating, self-harm, or suicidal behaviors, gestures, or threats.

i call my father to ask if what my brother says is right.

my father isn't using his real voice

so he says things he should not,

like what he really thinks.

he isn't using his real voice

because his hands are over his mouth

holding my hands.

it isn't hiding.

it's that afterwards i can't remember what just happened.

i call home to ask if there is still a sturdy girl there.

my mother says we are waiting to make it

to the end of the day

and asks me to come home.

enter character in search of a past

say the body dismembers. un-members.
say body.

entering the house there are two people
in the hallway. if disease is a testable
condition pills toward the still grieving
parts. say not mine but mine is not
separated either. leaving the house the
iron steps are shadows and descent is a
consequence of faith.

say fight, say crossing over.
say nightingale.

if you braced a megaphone to the neck
you might hear wanting before the
preposterous question of how. i hope it
rains today because i hope for the sound
of water arriving.

ask of our.
ask of your hollow heart.

say heart.

**a box is a container
and a comment on containment**

there is fire and the need of fire.

there is fire clearing the crowding near the streams.

there is fire and there is heat and the heat of the fire opens the seeds.

the ground is a fertile and burning place.

depending on the view there is devastation.

depending on the view the ground is covered in ash.

agencies begin to control the fire. agencies begin to control the where of fire. agencies control fire to correct their own effects on drowning and crowding by the streams.

the fires grow larger than the agencies intended. the fires reach the gates around the agencies. the streams are damaged and there is drowning.

the agencies return to control their own creations with water and more water and everything is wet, too wet to begin again.

agencies have built a place they call the natural world. the natural world has its weeds poisoned and curtains pulled over the machinery.

there is a boat. it isn't visible but that doesn't mean we don't get on it. sitting and dropping the faces on the boat all look different than they did before. some mouths spread open and scream. some take deep breaths while ascending. many close their eyes but none keep them closed. the ebb accelerates. we watch the falling trees with wide eyes. we watch the mountains falling.

no matter how many times we've been on the boat, we never know where we are going. we prepare for turns that take us upward and drop.

we are both separate and inseparable from one another.

we are a contradiction and barely surviving, and near us burns a ring around the fallen.

around the rings are the structures which are ours as much as they are not. highways are built through the middle. objects and hills are claimed into ownership. ownership is taken into the hands of banks whose vaults are filled with other people's currency, but not all of it. if everyone went looking for what was theirs, and took it back, there wouldn't be enough for everyone and some would have to give up pieces of what they believe is theirs. we are not willing to do that, made of separateness and inseparability.

orientation is not about north/south or left/right. it's about bodies and space. we don't notice orientation until we are disoriented. we are oriented in an already familiar world where north and south already exist. it is not about how to find our way but about how we come to feel at home.

the effects of inhabitance include how we face this home and how it is reachable and proximate. or not.

the familiar is shaped by actions that reach toward objects that are already within reach.

these homes are the histories of arrival. failures of extension. it is not controlled. but we are controlled. by the structures and the systems. how we begin, how we arrive, from which side. how here and there appear. where we dwell.

say economies and red. say ecologies and erasure.

the fact that something is written down does not make it true. it means that someone with sufficient authority to write things down recorded their version of events, of transactions, while someone else did not. it is evidence of some of what they did and some of what they wanted others to think they did.

when we rely on written records we must ask ourselves what might be missing, what might have been recorded in order to manipulate events. in what direction and in what ways do we allow ourselves to assume that objectivity is in any way connected with we are very happy to be here. we claw at pieces of tar across our mouths and spit.

when it is our turn to speak a kind of breaking happens. a kind of breaking. heads turn toward us and a kind of breaking happens. we look down. a breaking happens and we look down. we do not look up, willing away water. when it is our turn to speak say break.

we have our hands grabbed.

we have no instinct.

we don't want agencies to redistrict themselves to let us in. we want agencies to let us in without keeping other parts of us out.

we want water that holds, in which we wrap together and sleep.

yesterday when we talked about it, we spent the day trying to get farthest away from whoever it was that was closest. when we were touched we forgot the urge to recoil.

enter character whispering

we move along the edges of a body
of water at night. even if it isn't
night there is no discernible dis-
tance across. occasionally we sink
deeper, but do not submerge. stag-
nant water, covered in scum and al-
ways a body along the edge.

people know when they are taking
something from you.

the agencies are made out of concrete and brick. we walk among them. we walk within them. we are infected. curtains are pulled across the machinery. we are infected, but not all of us, not yet.

the agencies rely on inheritance, as in we are given what was never ours as a perpetuation of private property. a family is designed to stay closed-in behind walls. all that upward mobility or lack thereof. in one place agencies are spending thirteen billion on new cages and in another twelve on cracking the crust that is covered with concrete. somewhere someone we love grows ill and so we sign away choices to the whitest buildings. the agencies exhaust us. and we're exhausted from all the not-dreaming, but it is a requirement if there is anything else to be imagined. how to hold on across what won't appear in legal documents.

in the darkness we go to a quieter room. we did not choose because we cannot call it off if it becomes too hard. we do not choose because we cannot call it off.

but we choose because we've found each other.

enter character in search of a past

on the coast a figure pulling a shopping
cart no shoulder no face the face
covered in white it is almost dark do not
stop will she sleep in the road eyes catch
may not be all human bandaged face
no face cliffs the water pulling shoeless
something other worldly it is not safe
and someone says she wanders the coast
the face masked in white no one says
no face no one says stop and so no one
stops no holes or holes for eyes holes
masked in white masked in white a face
in the dark no face

enter characters surrounded by pink

and if we liked it as we were pinned down but never asked and again we were pinned down and usually like it when others use their big voices over our own because we don't like the sounds from our mouths. who have we learned this from and also there can't just be one shape of responsible, not just agencies or luck or genetic code. we all get taught somewhere along the way and the tether is decipherable on only some of our bodies. a sure sign is starting to believe what is said about you. next comes keeping secret that you believe it. and the woman screaming in the street has this tremendous power, see how everyone quiets and makes wide circles around her. and say she were one of our own. we quiet. we quiet the room.

enter character dressed in green

inheritance comes from all directions. whole neighborhoods defined against one another. bootstraps across heaving evidence. there is a thing called pushed. it is inside the mouth. surrogate is inside the mouth, even when it is not. in an iron field we want to make syllables to wanting and say doubt is like the fog. we have letters and witnesses and still question our own remembering.

just because there are no scars does not mean there are no marks.

is it worth reconfiguring the narrative if it becomes unrecognizable. is it worth saying, we still look exactly as we always have.

my mother says this time
she won't get on the boat at all.

i am far enough to know what she means,
but close enough not to believe her.

enter character carrying a book

under stress conditions, from either physical or emotional causes, sympathetic impulses to most visceral effectors increase greatly and cause them to respond in ways which enable the body to put forth its greatest physical effort, to expend its maximal amount of energy. in fact, one of the very first steps in the body's complex defense mechanism against stress is a sudden and marked increase in sympathetic activity.

enter character whispering

our clothes were wet but it was not raining.

the girl who used to become an animal screamed until we had to tie her arms and put her underwater.

we were just so young and didn't know who to tell, so we told no one.

about the girl and her howling.

enter character in search of a past

we are dreaming again. the others have been told not to wake us, that waking is a sign of the times. one of us wakes and begins to pull waves from her lips. she says, look at all i have brought you. she speaks to an empty room.

separated like this it's hard to imagine a whole. the houses are underwater and the organs are turning grey. we go home and have one but we're choking.

enter character in search of a past

the woman yelling on the street
has tremendous power.

she came in asking for the cup of the
day which isn't the kind of place it is
and ten dollars well that's a whole meal
how about a cup of coffee go ahead and
sit someone will be right over no i like to
carry it myself a stain beside the cross
laying near her heart and a slowness to
the walk that suggested attention beside
the door she lifts her hands as if every
muscle and synapse were slowed the
room disappears except all the hairs on
the arm are standing upright she sits
after exact change is taken from the
hand that smelled acrid and familiar
with not so many safe places to sleep she
mutters and turns her hand to the roof
and her head upward watching all the
whispers her back is turned and then
she is gone how many people disappear
bags set on the bench her finger on the
release valve of the lighter flame open
cigarette backwards it's backwards
she turns it around slowly and looks
into the sky looks into the sky talking.

the woman yelling on the street
has tremendous power.

and also she has none.

enter character whispering

when i was a girl the telephone would
ring and because she'd been calling
often my mother would say you answer
our voices sound alike i'd never heard a
threat over the phone but it was a word
i recognized it was my mother's name
she's not home i don't know when i
have to go and then my father picked
up and because our voices sounded
alike hello hello hello

enter character in search of a past

at the doctor's office the family history
slides down the page and off onto the floor.
when the little boy was nine she crossed the
ocean with no return ticket calling herself
a queen. doctors say every break takes you
a little farther from what you once were. the
phone rings and at night we wonder who
has flown where and what the children will
turn out to be. animals, when afraid for
their lives begin to shake, but emerge from
freezing with the same terror they entered
it. we are animals, but we are more afraid of
the shaking and the emerging than we are
of staying frozen, even when it is not winter.
people walk around looking like they are
flying above the ocean, like the boy holding
a hand of a stranger in a mother's body,
afraid of thawing. and after, there aren't as
many ways to think into what came before.

sometimes hyper-vigilance is the thing
inherited.

this is a story:

my mother's air gets rough two feet from her body.

give or take the time of year and her blood sugar count.

this is another story:

going home, i was the only one returning.

my father says, i'm not sorry he isn't here.

we can hear he is angry from the waves in his voice.

he says, i'm not sorry.

what it means to build a wall across a road of family.

this is a story:

survival is a state of existence that implies a constant presence

inside a situation that threatens it; a proximity to not surviving.

we are each carrying seven generations and wonder,

where is the way out.

toward the water we arrive halfway but don't go.

it's colder so we stay still, now.

whatever it is that we are dealing with

it is hard to see from any location.

there are things that can be understood.

and things that cannot.

we know this, but never had any experts who told us so.

did something happen to you?

it happened to all of us.

enter characters surrounded by pink

below certain lines internal organs give out at an average rate of ten years earlier than expected. statistics, even, have opinions. say disease and mean economy. say stable and mean afraid of loss. say how to love across illnesses that make people unloveable. i dreamt someone i loved had been seen walking in a desert talking to himself. say, how to care at the edges of everything is just fine.

none of these are the worst cases or the contexts that break. but there is so much breaking and so much drowning. we counted down in the rain until morning. but we changed courses because we had come wanting to talk of exceptions.

we are now beginning to recognize the shouting as our own.

there is wanting

there is a patient.

in their hands
is an object.
the object has weight.
the weight is spread
and sinewed.
the sinews are fragile,
not to be released
from a high location.
a feathered crack
running down
toward a base.
a base made supine
from captivity.

in their hands
there are often objects.
they wear them
or they carry them.

there is a patient.
the patient has been
taken hold of
and has taken hold.

it felt like they were climbing
and growing legs
they hadn't needed before.

there is a patient.

they lay looking
at the underpass
and waiting
for a good reason
to say yes
to another set
of somebodies.

the patient's hands get cold
with all this carrying,
and even colder
when everybody says,
look how empty
their hands are.

when the patient's father
came to see them
on the other edge
he was smaller
than they'd remembered.

the patient and the father
walk toward the other edge
where there are vertical forests
and different words for the wings
in the throat. beneath the trees
everything is small.

the patient
and their father
begin to see patterns.
vertical limbs,
worn and tethered,
having fallen
and a circle of newly emerged
surrounding what once was.

they begin to see patterns of fire.
and of what was lost
but not altogether lost.

the patient's father
slowly climbs the hill
and leans sideways
examining the hollowed creek.
he says, how such a beast
might be held and standing,
it must be those many others
that hold its leaning.
he says, tenuous roots
are tended by fire.

beside the hollows
the patient stands
in their ill-fitting skin.
the patient looks up and turns,
breathing heavy,
and their father
grows older.

the patient and their father
walk together up the hill
and enter a house.
and a thick trunk
reaches sideways
from the wall
of the hollowed creek bed.

this isn't mine to tell. and what is mine to tell includes the parts i don't want to expose. because i can't figure out what the cost is. and who it costs. because being a patient and not being a patient do not make a story. because all of us are patients and some of us are more patients than others. because i am more and less a patient depending on the view. depending on the company and location. because this is not a story and telling it won't help. or it will. and because a sibling who became a stranger and this not being the first time this has happened in these families is not a story. it is a history of stories recorded and forgotten and remembered. that there was hardly a beginning and having an end in sight not being a luxury we've ever afforded and yet we are still imagining endings and beginnings. which leads to my sense of not being able to tell what is mine and is not mine. which means i have illnesses that lay in my skin but that aren't visible in texts. which means there may be causes but the causes might be exactly what sustains us. or what we believe sustains us. which means i keep leaning away from this telling. because everything is dangerous and staying still everything is still dangerous. so dangerous that the worst might happen. or it won't but instead we might move through all the chokings and the crackings and even then we still might not know exactly how to love across the illnesses. what isn't mine to tell is also what i return to, unable to untell. that i have a brother who is ill, the kind of ill that spins in the night and the kind of ill that means at any moment i will set down everything i am holding and go find him or go looking. which means there is a kind of hatred for him. which means i will never know what it means to love a sibling in reciprocity. which means i expect to care for and not to be cared for. which has everything to do with the body i was born with. and this does not make a story because this is the kind of story that implicates us all. because these illnesses aren't personal. they are illnesses that are the very fabrics of the agencies that we walk amongst and the chemicals that make us and the ways our grandparents treated other grand-parents and how they treated everyone before and after. living inside the natural world built by agencies and having a body that i am told is not my own and having a brother who is ill but is also doing fine is not a way of telling but a way of seeing. and because i cannot see enough the story is wrought with contradiction and indignation and shame. which leads to my sense of not being able to tell what is, and is not, mine. like how we all carry inside of us what came before us and lingers around us. like how i carry inside me the story of my father when he was nine years old as he rode on a boat across the canal carrying his drunken father. how he went looking for the doctor aboard the ship and the doctor came and examined the liver and the lights were few on the water and my father was alone on a boat and very, very small and while my father has never told me this story, i remember this story. that this is how my father learned to speak. and because there will always be a veil between us that stands in the place of language, there is also a veil necessary to looking back and seeing him so small. he's always been afraid, as i am, wanting to pull down the veils and not being able to, for fear of being seen. knowing this is not a story. the agencies tell the stories about the ones who are quiet and the ones who are sick and the ones who are evil depending on the placement of their bodies. how i was driving by looking out the window and did not stop. how many times did i go by and never stop, feeling worried and afraid and implicated and never telling anyone that i didn't want to have the feeling of knowing so much and never telling anyone that i was planning on disappearing so as to not have to pick up any more metaphorical pieces.

i haven't told the story of being in and beside and surrounded and choked by illnesses that have no symptoms but are nonetheless of the body, that have no origins but are nonetheless originating in how and what is eaten, or breathed in, as much as it originates in all the bodies that led down or across or up to us. we can never stop telling this story as much as we try to. once i was a woman. once i was a woman who carried a child to the river as it screamed. as it could not stop screaming with its belly swelling up. screaming and swelling and how i loved it across the screaming. and there was no doctor to come. i had the screaming that would not stop and so i sent the other children to the barn and told them to sleep and carried the swelling and screaming to the river. how i held the screaming and loved through the screaming and placed the screaming in the water. placed the screaming in the water as the final act of love. how i've never lost my breath in water. how i remember all this but do not remember it. like how i've never carried anything in my arms. like how i remember all this and did not experience it, but that doesn't mean it isn't mine and it doesn't mean it doesn't happen in other ways everyday. how a river and a street and a highway are symbols of things. how we don't want agencies to hear us, or let us in without letting other parts of us in. how we are separated and how many times have we been reborn beside a river. and how when my brother sends a letter saying the night is spinning i begin to act, not just hear the spinning or the screaming. and how i do not tell anyone because it might alarm them. just hold the alarm, as i've seen my mother do. and do not tell anyone because i have come to believe that illnesses too arise out of psychic wounds. there are so many ways. like remembering being beside a river. and not having been beside the river. like having a mother with a sister who called saying her name as a threat. who got in a plane holding a little boy by the hand. like having a father who carried his drunken father across a canal. like having a body that i am told is mine when others are told their bodies are not their own. like having a body that i am told is not mine when others are told their bodies are their own. how none of this is outside the body if the body doesn't end at the skin. how choice is a deception, when the choices are between one way of curdling cells and another. when it is at its most quiet i worry what happens as things are left alone to spin and what happens when we no longer see ourselves as parts of one another. which is a very complex thing. which requires stages and scenes and telling and not telling. i haven't told because there is only one story to tell and we could tell it in all of our voices so as long as no one's voice is silenced. i haven't told because i am afraid all this telling won't amount to much. just a tree climbing through the walls of the house and blooming through the ceiling. and so it is. we lean against each other's arms and are glass bottles. by this i mean: it is always more than what it looks like.

in the forest the patients have a strange sensation of shapes shifting, larging and smalling. faces curled toward theirs. a billowy body in a bed and even the feet when they press against are forgotten. outside they are also in this bed and this bed is like other beds along the highways. then the horizon is search lights and signs for not killing the living things inside and the patients begin to cry. because how the patients and the others around them wanted to see the world turning is not how it continues to turn. and they're older now so the pressures have mounted but so has the grief. what to do with their shells being less dense now. the patients' skins shred as they admit that it has become harder to know where in the body the urge to say something resides. they don't tell stories at night, even when others ask them to. and the closeness here in the forest is also the closeness to water and then it is fully night. the patients turn around and continue to where the candles are lit. they watch the flies light on the low trees until the moon rises red. the press of their faces upon other faces and smalling and larging. their eyelids get heavy and the red moon rises. smoke begins quietly and already, there are songbirds.

this is a story: the sky is wild and we watch it.

what passes by the window is really the window passing by the unmoving things. and so nothing is unmoving. we're leaving, unmarked and changed. and what about what to do after.

of course we are disoriented. we can't tell north from south. we have only known where we were in the already familiar world.

this is a story: we watch the wild sky whimper.

it was then we felt born into water. we were taken, still wrinkled, to the shore to look across toward where we could barely begin to see. and the beats of our heart is unsteadied and labored.

in the forest, there are bodies. there are these bodies. bodies reaching and fallen bodies. there are bodies that emerge when a birthing body is damaged, injured, or diseased. there are fallen bodies that are also reaching, a single limb extending for as much as two hundred feet toward water.

when the fallen are consumed by the very flames that open new seeds there forms a ring of new torsos bursting upward from webbed beneath. bursting which lasts years and is invisible to the eye. although there are many who see.

there are these bodies leaning and holding and these hands outstretched.

enter character carrying a book

what is it if it is not a love story.

enter characters

the sky is wild and we watch it.

afterward:
in the beginning there were endings, too

we arrive as precarious bodies. and being precarious we aren't sure we matter. but we know that some acts of arrival make others appear. and we are precarious beneath the unhinging structures and in composition against the metal horizons. and so we are precarious among a tangle of climbing and drying and growing legs.

we walk on pavement. we notice how we've forgotten motion in its undecided terms. when we look there are sturdy roots that we've begun to recognize as growing beneath. and all around us are sets of stories and fires and breathing.

in these times we feel a drowning coming on. we would like to stop it but we are being touched from more directions than we can look in such a hurry. in these times we ask for silence and we begin to fall. perhaps the best that can be done is to give systematic chaos the articulations of characters with almost visible shadows.

and so we begin to untell a set of stories. we wake up with thirst. we begin to notice when wanting arrives and we reach the hands. we point to the places in the torso where old habits grow tired of not being useful anymore. we notice, too, the resistance to release, but when the body lets go it becomes a buoyant piece and floats.

and so water tends to a boundary-less shore. we're not sure we matter, or if not mattering is a disruption to the saying, but we'd like to say anyway that the smallest kind of noticing makes a difference. and then the rooms buzz with laughter. here grows a shoreline. the shoreline carries nightingale. say nightingale.

we're not sure we matter, having crossed over the bounds between sea and shore. or if anyone saying that we matter changes anything, but at any rate we'd like to say that in exit a rhythm to water not unlike an ebb. the shoreline has its own set of impulses that originate with the lack of beginnings. we want to know what happens and if we matter. but we are positive now that the not mattering doesn't matter much. or that we might just be a suggestion of how.

and so we begin again. we begin again despite the storms. there is always the choice to swim. there is always the choice to swim with all the rest of the bodies covered in skin and water and skin and water. and it has taken all we had to arrive. and so we arrive swimming. toward a shore. or toward where the shore no longer matters.

borrowed language, formative materials and guidance were found in the following places:

1971 textbook of *anatomy and physiology* by catherine parkery anthony and norma jane kolthoff; m. jacqui alexanders's *pedagogies of crossing;* john landreau's *notes on sara ahmed's queer phenomenology;* rebekah edwards' guidance toward affect theory and in particular: elspeth probyn's *eating skin,* erin manning's *the politics of touch,* joan scott's *the evidence of experience,* and aurora levins morales' *historian as curandera; trauma stewardship* by laura van dernoot lipsky; *somatic engagement* edited by petra kuppers, obsessive internet research on borderline personality disorder; wikipedia's definitions of disease; my inbox; the disability justice movement; the icarus project; long conversations in kitchens with charles arpe and monica gomery; telephone calls and winding roads with sean gleason. this book is dedicated to s and j, who know more than they should about a story that is also theirs. and if nothing else, this is a love story i hope he never reads.

Tessa Micaela Landreau-Grasmuck was born in Philadelphia and currently resides in Oakland with her dog, Ramona Pickle. Tessa has waited tables, bound books, worked as an abortion counselor, reproductive health educator, and birth doula, taught writing in the San Francisco county jail, studied herbalism, and carved out time to write between it all. Tessa was granted the first Community Poetics Fellowship from Mills College, where she received her MFA in 2013. Tessa is the author of the chapbook *Crude Matter* (ypolita press, 2015). Other writing has appeared in Make/shift, Dusie, Open House, Sink Review, and various other jars and corners. *there are boxes and there is wanting* is her first book.